HIGH-FIVE FINANCES

FIVE WAYS TO REACH YOUR FINANCIAL GOALS

HAMP LEE III

(com)mission™
PUBLISHING

High-Five Finances: Five Ways to Reach Your Financial Goals
Hamp Lee III. 1st ed.

ISBN: 1940042313
ISBN 13: 978-1940042312

TABLE OF CONTENTS

INTRODUCTION

The high five: a gesture where you slap the palm of your hand against the palm of another person's hand in the air. It's an act that provides instant acknowledgment of an achievement or exhilaration relating to a specific task or event. Sadly, however, when it came to my finances, I probably deserved a slap across the head rather than a high five.

Growing up, I had one rule of money management: if money was in my pocket, I was going to spend it. I wanted instant gratification by having fun with my friends.

When I entered the military, I had only twenty dollars in my pocket. Though I would soon earn more money than I ever had before, my financial habits didn't change. Within five years, I had been in and out of debt several times because of my decisions. After a friend talked to me about investing, I started saving a very small percentage of my income. I knew it wasn't enough to meet my financial goals, but I figured saving something was better than nothing at all.

Though I can't claim to be a millionaire after serving twenty years in the military, I have a lot more now than the twenty dollars I started with. Through many hard lessons, I've developed better spending habits to reach my financial goals. I've been able to condense these lessons into five steps and share them with you.

High-Five Finances: Five Ways to Reach Your Financial Goals is a simple five-step guide to help you get a better handle on your finances. Throughout this book, I'll share how I gained greater control of my finances, along with a few principles to help you build or improve your financial standing.

In sharing my life of financial failures and successes, I hope to spare you from years of mistakes and financial ruin. Regardless of your current financial situation, I believe it's never too late to get your finances in order. By learning more about your spending habits and expenses, you can build a financial plan to not only protect yourself and your family, but also budget and invest toward your financial goals.

KNOW YOURSELF

Financial management is not about finding the quickest route, plan, or scheme to make a million dollars. Sound financial management is having the proper discipline to execute a plan to meet specific financial goals within a specified time frame. And in order to reach your goals, you must first know where you are.

POINT A

Moving from your financial Point A to Point B is much like using a GPS system. To reach a specific destination, your GPS must first identify your current position. Without a starting point, your GPS cannot plot a route specific to your predetermined options. Proper money management is no different.

In order to have a successful financial plan, you must understand where you are as well as the decisions, behaviors, and habits that got you there. This encompasses your Point A. Understanding your Point A will help you learn the *why* and *how* of your financial decisions in order to create a tailor-made plan based on your spending background, history, and habits.

To help you understand more about your Point A, I've prepared a financial questionnaire. The purpose of this questionnaire is to uncover your relationship with money, track your spending habits, and detail your current financial standing.

Using a notebook, word-processing program, or app, take a few moments to answer the following questions. Please keep your responses in one location because you'll return to them in future chapters.

STARTING OFF

Write a summary of your current financial health. Describe your spending habits, how you manage your finances each month, the state of your current debt and bills, your method for paying your bills, and the amount of time you've sought to improve your finances.

CHILDHOOD EXPERIENCES

1. Growing up, did anyone teach you about money management? If so, who was it (parent, grandparent, family friend, personal friend, etc.)?

2. If you received a weekly or biweekly allowance, how long did it typically take to spend the entire amount? (Select one and explain.)

     a. 0–24 hours

     b. 25–48 hours

     c. 48–72 hours

     d. a week or longer

3. Did you save or invest any portion of your allowance?

4. If you saved a portion of your allowance, what did you save your money for?

a. emergencies

b. a large purchase or gift

c. a special event

d. a holiday or birthday

e. other (please explain)

5. Did you have to work to support your family (help pay bills, purchase food, etc.)? (If yes, please explain.)

6. Did you typically spend your allowance or paycheck to purchase the latest shoes, clothing, games, smartphones, or other non-necessities? (If yes, please explain.)

7. What did you typically purchase with your allowance or paycheck? (Prioritize all applicable items and explain.)

a. food

b. movies/entertainment

c. games or apps

d. clothing or shoes

e. items for family and/or friends

f. other (explain)

SPENDING HABITS

1. Since childhood, how would you describe your spending habits?

    a. a lot better

    b. slightly better

    c. slightly worse

    d. a lot worse

2. As an adult, do you regularly purchase the latest shoes, clothing, games, smartphones, electronics, or other non-necessities? (If yes, please explain.)

3. In the last five years, how many vehicles have you owned?

    a. 0–1 vehicle(s)

    b. 2–4 vehicles

    c. 5 or more vehicles

4. If you have an auto loan, what percentage of your monthly income do you spend paying it?

    a. 1–5 percent

    b. 6–10 percent

    c. 11–15 percent

    d. 16–20 percent

    e. 21 percent or more

5. What percentage of your monthly income do you spend paying your current bills (rent, utilities, phone, insurance, etc.)?

    a. 0–10 percent

    b. 11–20 percent

    c. 21–30 percent

    d. 31–40 percent

    e. 41 percent or more

6. Reviewing your last bank statement, how much money did you spend on the following items? If you don't have a bank account, track your spending in the categories below for the next thirty days.

    a. eating out (fast-food and dine-in restaurants)

    b. personal care (hair, nails, massages, etc.)

    c. electronics (games, apps, headphones, etc.)

    d. alcohol

    e. attending festivals, concerts, movies, clubs, or other activities

    f. clothing and shoes

7. In the last sixty days, how much money did you save for emergencies, your children's college fund, vacations, and/or retirement?

8. Have you ever purchased items based on emotion or impulse (car, holiday gifts, etc.)? (If yes, please explain.)

9. Do you purchase expensive items for birthdays, holidays, anniversaries, and other celebratory days throughout the year? (If yes, please explain.)

10. Do you typically buy something because it's on sale, even if you don't need it? (If yes, please explain.)

11. Do you buy items at large sales held throughout the year, including the holidays (i.e., Black Friday)? If so, what is the average amount you spend during each outing?

12. Of the four spending profiles below, which one (or more) would describe you, and why:

a. Nickel-and-Dimer: Spends money on small items as long as there's money in the account.

b. Big Spender (lite): Spends money on expensive items, but not often.

c. Big Spender (heavy): Nickel-and-Dimer and Big Spender (lite) combined; purchases expensive items often.

d. Penny Pincher: Slow to purchase anything unless absolutely necessary.

BANK ACCOUNTS
AND CREDIT CARDS

1. How many bank accounts do you currently have? If you have more than two, please explain the purpose of each account.

2. Looking at your last three bank statements (or months), how much money has been in your bank account on the day prior to receiving your next paycheck?

3. How many credit and department store cards do you currently have? Please describe the credit limit of each card, along with your current balance and interest rate.

4. If you have a savings account, what is your current balance? Are you pleased with this amount? If not, please explain why, and provide your ideal savings amount.

PAYING BILLS

1. Have you ever been late in paying your bills? (If yes, please explain.)

2. Typically, do you pay the minimum balance on your credit and department store cards and loans, or do you pay more than the required amount?

3. If your employer were unable to pay you for one month, would you be able to cover your current bills? If not, how would you get the money to pay these bills?

4. Have your habits caused any of your bills or debts to be turned over to a collection agency? (If yes, please explain.)

CREDIT REPORT

1. When was the last time you reviewed your credit report?

2. Do you currently have any negative entries on your credit report because of a failure to pay a bill or debt? (If yes, please explain.)

3. Have you ever filed for bankruptcy? If so, please explain the circumstances leading to your filing.

RELATIONSHIPS

If you're in a relationship,

1. Do you have separate or joint banking and/or investment accounts? (Please explain.)

2. If you have separate banking and investment accounts, do you assign the payment of bills equally? Please explain your current arrangement.

3. Do you and your partner regularly discuss your financial standing and specific goals? (If yes, please explain.)

4. Looking back at question #12 under Spending Habits, which spending profile(s) would best describe your partner?

5. Do you believe your partner's spending or financial perspective has helped or hurt your joint financial goals? (Please explain.)

POINT B

Now that you have a better understanding of your Point A, let's talk about Point B. Your Point B represents your financial goals. These goals can address your financial needs in the next five minutes or thirty years, and be as broad, varied, or specific as you desire. As you consider what your Point B may look like, incorporate the following two guidelines.

First, regardless of the goals you establish, please ensure each one is SMART. SMART goals are Specific, Measurable, Achievable, Realistic, and Time-focused. A SMART goal can be as simple as saying, "In the next thirty days, I would like to save one hundred dollars and place the money in a savings account." This goal is SMART because it's specific and measurable (saving one hundred dollars in a savings account), achievable and realistic (based on my current financial situation), and time-focused (within thirty days).

Second, establish goals for the short-term (one to six months), the midterm (seven months to two years), and the long-term (two years or longer). Some goals (especially long-term goals) may not seem as SMART, but write them down anyway. Also, consider the steps you may need to take to bring them to fruition.

For example:

Thirty days: Reduce eating out in half.

Six months: Save $_____ in a savings account to cover bills for one month or an emergency (using the money saved from eating out less).

One year: Pay off one bill.

Two years: Pay off a second bill.

Three years: Pay off all bills, save $_____ per month for your children's college education, and/or invest $_____ each month.

Four years: Purchase your first home.

Please spend the next several days considering your Point B. Use your current life circumstances, work situation, and savings as your starting point. Include your partner in this goal-setting process as well.

Once you establish your goals, you may need to adjust them as you continue reading this book and as situations in your life change. Seasons of life often bring unexpected events that adjust or delay your financial goals, and that's okay. Be flexible so you can properly address the specific situation(s) in front of you, and when you're ready or able, return to your (readjusted) goals.

NEWS REPORTING

Now that you've had an opportunity to discover a little more about your financial history, spending habits, and future financial goals, let's take a deeper look at where your money goes each month. In order to do this, you'll need a financial compass.

A financial compass is similar to a standard compass, which provides an accurate heading in a specific direction. However, instead of using direction markers for north, south, east, and west, a financial compass uses Needs, Everything in-between, Wants, and Savings (NEWS). Identifying your NEWS will help you determine whether you're moving closer to or further from your Point B.

NEEDS

Your needs are mandatory items that are absolutely necessary for day-to-day survival, such as food, clothing, or housing. Bills should also be included in this category because of the importance of fulfilling your financial obligations.

Bills are payments you make to various entities for services you initiate. Whether it's a rent payment, utilities, phone service, or credit card charges, you commit yourself to short- and long-term financial agreements. If you were to categorize some of your bills, however, they would probably fit in one of the next two categories.

EVERYTHING IN-BETWEEN

Everything in-between are *comfort* items that typically improve or enhance your daily living, such as vacations, eating out, television, movies, and hobbies. Though these are neither needs nor wants, they may be closer to wants.

WANTS

Wants are items that satisfy your pleasures and desires. Emotional impulse often drives their purchase.

SAVINGS

Your savings includes any amount you set aside or save in a bank account from your monthly paycheck(s) or other sources of income. You can use the money you save for an emergency, unexpected event, or for any other purchase. Your savings is separate from what you invest into mutual funds, stocks, bonds, Individual Retirement Accounts (IRAs), and/or 401(k) accounts.

NEWS REPORTING

In order to provide a report on your NEWS, you'll need to itemize, track, and categorize your expenses. As an exercise, let's start with your expenses from last month. Use your responses from the previous chapter to assist you.

When ready, record each of your expenditures into one of the four NEWS categories. When categorizing your bills, make a side note for each expenditure that may fit into Everything in-between or Wants. After you consolidate your purchases in their respective NEWS categories, list the total amount for each category. When complete, answer the following questions:

1. What are your initial thoughts about the amount of money you've spent in each area?

2. In which category did you spend the largest amount of money? Least? Which category surprised you the most?

3. For the purchases in Everything in-between and Wants, explain your reason for making each purchase. (Also include expenditures listed in Needs that may fit into Everything in-between or Wants.) Do the reasons for your purchases relate back to your childhood? If so, explain how.

4. How has your spending helped or hurt your ability to reach your Point B?

Maybe you're like many of us who never considered the consequences of our spending, who are so focused on enjoying life today that we sacrifice our needs for tomorrow. But armed with more information about yourself and the direction of your spending, you can change your current heading. You can use what you've learned to adjust your spending by changing your relationship with the stuff you want and the stuff you already own.

BEING CONTENT

"What I have already is enough."

Take a moment to consider all of the stuff you currently own: clothes, shoes, and electronics are just the beginning. Think about the amount of money you spent to have the latest smartphone, although you had just purchased one several months prior, or the pair of jeans that were twenty percent off but are similar to the three pair you already own.

I've been there, done that...and much more. My reason for buying so much (or at least wanting so much) came from a lack of contentment. Though I owned something that was working well and in good shape, I still felt the need to buy the newest and latest items. This is probably a major reason why I remained in debt for so long. I allowed the pursuit of *better* and *newer* stuff (I didn't need) to keep me in debt and further from my Point B.

Several years ago, I purchased a fifty-six-inch television. As the technology vastly improved over the years, I finally had an urge to purchase a new seventy-inch television. Nothing was wrong with the fifty-six-inch television, but my contentment waned because it didn't have the latest technological features. I started justifying (to my wife and myself) why I needed a bigger, fancier television, even though the fifty-six-inch television had been nothing but stellar.

In the end, I couldn't justify purchasing a new television other than saying, "I want it." To reach that decision, I had to address my emotional impulses in order to understand that what I already owned was enough.

The seventy-inch television was neither the first nor the last item I'll want to purchase. My contentment may wane in another area, and I'll have to be just as prepared to ensure that I think with my head and not with my emotions.

A PLACE OF CONTENTMENT

Reaching a place of contentment in the heat of a potential purchase is more about controlling your emotions, thinking logically, and keeping your financial goals in mind. You can't have all the stuff you want and your Point B at the same time. There's going to be a trade-off somewhere. Sacrifice will be necessary, and for many of us, that has been our Point B.

When I bought *better* and *newer* stuff, I often used them as a means to gain greater acceptance, to make me feel happier, and seem more important. Because these things never helped me reach a place of true contentment, I kept spending, hoping the next item would fill that void, but it never did. I had to understand that things cannot bring true happiness, and what I have is all I need.

Dealing with your emotional impulses may not be easy, but it's absolutely necessary if you want to reach your financial goals. The example I gave about the seventy-inch television took me two weeks to work through. I would think off and on about buying the television for several days. Then, just when I thought I had come to a final decision not to purchase the television, I would see something similar at a store or in a commercial, and would go through the same roller coaster of emotions all over again. However, I continued working through a series of questions to help me move beyond my impulsive desires:

1. Is this something I need or want?

2. How would this purchase benefit my family or me?

3. Do I have enough money to pay for this item now? If not, how am I planning to pay for it?

4. Will this purchase help or hurt my family's financial standing and goals?

5. Is this purchase absolutely necessary for my family's current needs?

6. Do I already own something similar? If so, why or how would this item be any different? What's wrong with what I already own?

7. If I want to purchase this item to solve a problem I'm facing, is there a cheaper way to accomplish the same result?

When you're in the midst of a potential purchase driven by emotional impulse, you should consider similar questions and your Point B. With such a self-examination, you may find that what you own already is enough. And as you become more content with what you own, you'll have the opportunity to put more of your money to work toward reaching your Point B.

ENTERTAINMENT AND EATING OUT

Because many of us place a great importance on personal happiness, we often spare no expense on entertainment and eating out. Though entertainment and eating out allow us to feel loved, appreciated, and accepted, the cost of personal happiness can add up in a big way. I'm not saying you can't or shouldn't go out to eat or enjoy a bit of entertainment with your friends and family. I am saying that you should place a little more attention on your spending in these areas and find less expensive ways to have a good time.

About ten years ago, my family and I reduced our outings to the movies and rented videos instead. Each Friday, we rented a movie or two and bought a box of popcorn. We placed blankets and pillows in front of our television and enjoyed our evening together. We called it our campfire.

It was a bit hard, waiting for the movies we really wanted to see to come out on video, but saving over forty dollars per movie visit sounded a lot better. In the end, it was worth every bit of our patience. Not only did we save money, but we also created memorable moments along the way.

As another example, a few years ago, my family and I ate out at restaurants two times each week. Though we ate out only twice a week, we spent about $620 a month! When my daughter left for college, my wife and I stopped our weekly regimen and added a Saturday breakfast instead. At that point, we were spending about one hundred dollars each month. However, after one very poor experience at a restaurant, we decided to eat that meal at home as well.

For less than fifteen dollars, we purchased a box of pancake mix and two packs of deliciously thick bacon. The bacon lasted about three weeks, and the box of pancake mix lasted two months. Instead of spending two hundred dollars at a restaurant over a two-month period, we spent about thirty dollars (I needed more bacon). Plus, I could stay home in my pajamas and enjoy the company of my lovely wife.

HIGH-FIVE MOMENT

Before you continue reading any further, I'd like for you to try an another exercise. For the next thirty days, cut your eating and going out in half. Use your time to enjoy the company of friends and family without spending a lot of money. Play board games, draw, take a walk in the park, or sit on your porch and reminisce. After thirty days, describe your experiences and the ways in which you used any extra income.

The purpose of this exercise is to help you find less expensive ways to have a good time and squeeze a little extra income from your paycheck to save or invest. Not everyone can receive a pay raise or have a schedule that allows them take on a second job for more money. Restricting your spending is an easy way to give yourself the extra money you need for unexpected events and meeting your financial goals.

PROTECTING YOU FROM YOU

Within this chapter, you'll draw upon everything you've learned about yourself and your finances to develop a financial protection plan. A financial protection plan is a personalized plan based on your spending profile and monthly spending habits. It is a workable, realistic, and flexible plan to get your financial spending under control so you can begin working toward your Point B.

The financial protection plan I describe in the following pages is the process I used to gain greater control of my spending and financial health. After years of multiple attempts, I found five steps that worked for me, and I want to share them with you. Though these steps were beneficial for me, they may not be the best ones suited for you. Maybe you'll need an extra step or two...or possibly, fewer steps. But you should make sure your plan fits your circumstances and your financial needs and goals.

As you consider these five steps, review your answers from the previous chapters. Those answers are critical to how you build *your* financial protection plan.

1. ELIMINATE CAREFREE SPENDING

When I was growing up, going to the mall was a regular weekend occurrence with my friends. We didn't have a lot of money to spend, but it was a good place to walk around and hang out. But this created a bad habit.

As an adult, I continued my ritual of walking around malls and other department stores. The difference was that I now had the means to buy the things I wanted. Many times, I walked out of these stores with shopping bags in hand because I allowed my emotional impulses to get the best of me.

To change this pattern, I stopped walking in malls and department stores if I didn't have a specific reason to be there. Going to these stores only stirred my impulsive behavior. I had to become more content with the things I already owned.

In addition, I stopped participating in weekend and holiday sales throughout the year. I couldn't allow a thirty percent off Black Friday sale to drive me into a shopping frenzy. I couldn't allow the temptation to save on something I didn't need in the first place to get the best of me.

Along with ending my trips to malls and holiday sales, I also adjusted my ATM withdrawals. In the past, if I withdrew twenty dollars from the ATM and had change left over after a purchase, I often wasted it on things I didn't need—a pack of gum, chips and soda, or a magazine. Before I knew it, any remaining change was gone.

To address my carefree spending, I decided to withdraw money only when necessary. I also decreased the amount of money I carried with me. I used my debit card to purchase almost everything. This allowed me to be more purposeful with my spending and my finances as a whole.

Eating out multiple times in a week, going out multiple times, and purchasing frivolous items are small charges that add up quickly. Eliminating carefree spending can remove you from tempting situations or habits that eat up your income and decrease your ability to meet your financial goals.

2. REDUCE BIRTHDAY, ANNIVERSARY, AND HOLIDAY GIFTS

Consider the multitude of commercials and advertisements seeking to stimulate your emotional impulses to buy their wares. Almost daily, you're bombarded with *opportunities* to spend money without regard for how it affects you financially. On top of this, there are societal expectations and pressures to purchase expensive gifts as a means to show or gauge your affection for others. Through these internal and external *pressures*, you may spend thousands of dollars on gifts each year.

Reducing birthday, anniversary, and holiday gift giving can be a very sensitive and emotional process for many people. Dealing with your internal struggles, societal norms and customs, and expectations from your friends and family can be difficult. It'll be extremely important for you to address your internal concerns and communicate your desire to reduce the number and/or dollar amount of the gifts you purchase and why. Some of your friends and family members will be more understanding than others.

If you do decide to purchase gifts, consider placing them on your short- or midterm Point B, and save toward them rather than buying them on credit or taking out a loan. You can also purchase or make customized greeting cards and candy bags, or buy less expensive items such as popcorn or cookie tins so that you don't accumulate large amounts of debt.

3. ESTABLISH AN ALLOWANCE

A couple years ago, my wife suggested I receive an allowance. She said it would allow me to spend all I wanted within reason. As a self-proclaimed nickel-and-dimer, I thought I had a good handle on my spending already. But, after discussing it for about a week or so, she won out and I received my first allowance.

Within the first month, I realized I didn't have as good of a handle on my spending as I thought—we had a sizable amount of money left over. As a nickel-and-dimer, I was in the habit of buying little things throughout the month, without any concern for what it was doing to our finances. If money was in the account, I figured a dollar or two on a song download couldn't hurt. But over time, I guess it did. With the extra income, I immediately put it to work by making additional payments on bills, adding to our savings, and growing our investments.

Having an allowance taught me greater discipline in my spending. Because my wife included my gasoline in the allowance, I had to be more strategic in my spending. Outside of gasoline, I often purchased a few songs, an app or two, and at least one bobblehead (I'm a collector). I also saved up for a pair of shoes I wanted—something I had rarely done in the past. Though I no longer nickel-and-dime my way to buying everything I want, it feels good knowing our finances are getting healthier.

An allowance allows you to spend a limited amount of money on some of the things you want and need. It provides you with a greater perspective on not only your spending habits but whether certain purchases are even worth making. At best, an allowance helps you form a more judicious evaluation of your purchases.

Spend a little today, to save a lot more for tomorrow.

4. SAVE FOR EMERGENCIES

My introduction into the world of saving began with two mutual fund accounts. Though mutual funds are considered investments, I used these funds as *extended* savings accounts. I was really proud to save one hundred dollars each month. I felt like I deserved a high-five. It was a modern miracle.

The one thing I liked about the mutual fund accounts was that it took two or three days to withdraw any funds. Almost every time I thought about withdrawing funds to make a purchase, I found it rare to have a legitimate reason to proceed. The potential wait time gave me a chance to consider the legitimacy of any potential purchase.

Some people have the restraint to place their money under a mattress or in a savings account. Others will need to place their money in an account that's hard to reach or give it to a friend or family member they trust. There are numerous ways you can save, but the important thing is to start saving.

You know yourself and your spending habits. Create a method to protect you from you so you can have something saved for your future needs. As you build greater self-control and contentment, you can change your savings type in order to have options that are more accessible.

Today, I no longer have the mutual fund accounts. I simply use a savings account. I've adjusted my savings vehicle to match my improved spending discipline. Now I can have money immediately available to meet any specific need.

The amount you choose to save will vary from one person to the next. You can save enough to cover your bills for one month or one year. You can save five hundred dollars, one thousand dollars, or three to six months of your monthly income. Your savings goal should be what you believe will meet your needs for a specific event or period of time. Unexpected events do happen, so you want to be as prepared as possible. This is the essence of saving—having the ability to meet your needs when you need it most.

5. REDUCE DEBT

For years, I've owned only one credit card and no department store cards. I was afraid of having too many credit cards because, no matter what my credit limit was, I was always a few dollars away from the maximum credit limit. The reason my credit card bill was so high was that I used it to supplement my excessive spending. Instead of saving to purchase something I wanted (or not buying it at all), I charged it.

When it came to paying my credit card bill, I only paid the minimum amount due. Because the interest rate was more than the minimum payment, my balance wasn't decreasing. I was spending thousands of dollars to pay my credit card balance only to see it remain at the same level.

To correct this, I initially went to the opposite extreme. I started paying an excessive amount of money toward the credit card bill. Because I spent so much paying the bill, I ended up using the credit card to cover some of my expenses. Once again, I was back to a maxed-out card. After a month or two of this frustration, I adjusted my strategy. I paid an amount that was greater than the minimum amount due but wasn't so crushing to my day-to-day living that I would need to use the credit card again.

After paying several hundred dollars toward my balance, I would call the credit card company, asking to lower my credit card limit by five hundred dollars. Because I knew myself and my spending habits, I didn't lower it to the exact balance. I wanted a small buffer to cover any unexpected expenses because I only had a small amount in savings during this time. I continued this cycle until the credit card balance was at an amount I could reasonably pay within two paychecks.

This method of paying down my credit card bill is a bit unorthodox, and many would not recommend it. Each time I called, the credit card company stated that reducing my credit limit would negatively impact my credit rating. At the time, I wasn't concerned about my credit rating because I wasn't trying to use my credit to purchase anything else. My focus was on improving my financial standing. (In the end, my decision did not negatively impact my credit.)

How you choose to pay down your debt should be as personal as your circumstances and your financial abilities will allow. Don't worry about trying to pay off your bills as quickly as possible. Establish a plan based on your situation and follow it. Even if it takes a couple of years to pay down one bill, stay the course. Remain committed to building a financial protection plan that works for you. Take what you've learned and talk with your friends, family members, and even a financial counselor.

As you protect yourself from yourself, you may discover that the path toward your Point B is well within reach.

BE BIG

Many of us dream of having big financial accounts. We want the means to provide greater opportunities and options for ourselves and others in the future. In time, these opportunities and options can be ours, but it'll take a BIG mindset to make them a reality: Budget, Invest, and Give.

Budget to know where your money goes.

Invest to create future financial options.

Give to help others reach their Point B.

BUDGET

A budget is a very important part of your financial game plan. It helps you identify the income that comes in, and where and how it goes back out. A budget helps you stay on the path toward meeting your future financial goals.

In building your budget, it's important for your income to be placed into specific categories, such as rent, groceries, utilities, child care, savings, or even entertainment. When you categorize your spending, you have the ability to not only know where your money goes but also have historical data for each category.

After you establish your budget, review it throughout each pay period. Consider it your pre- and postgame reviews. In your pregame review, you'll build your budget as accurately as possible. Some categories have defined amounts (rent and car payment), and others will vary from month to month (utilities). In the case of varying bills or expenses, provide an average cost based on past billing statements and set aside a few dollars in savings for those occasional surges in spending. In your postgame review, return to your budget and provide actual amounts.

Based on your final totals, you may have more or less income remaining. If you have remaining income, you have a few options. One option is to leave the income in your account as a *buffer* to cover any overspending or other unexpected expenses. You also could place your remaining income in savings, investments, or make an extra payment on a bill. Whatever you decide to do with your remaining income, make sure you consider yourself, your family, and your Point B.

If you find that you're overspending, you can adjust your spending in one or more areas to balance your budget. For example, after a couple months, you find that you're going over budget and have to use your savings to cover your expenses. After reviewing your budget data, you see that your grocery bill has been a bit high. You decide to stick to your shopping list, but go to a different store to see if your bill lowers. After shopping at the new store, your grocery bill is not much lower. You now have the option of continuing to shop at the new store, or returning to the original store, with the understanding that your shopping list will need to be adjusted. If you decide not to trim your shopping list, you also have the option of adjusting another item on your budget.

Your goal in budgeting is not to overcommit or under commit your income. You want your budget to be just right —an intentional and purposeful tool for reaching your Point B.

INVEST

An investment is an asset or item that is purchased with the hope it will generate income or appreciate in the future. It is a means of increasing financial options.

There are multiple types of investments. Each type of investment comes with inherent benefits and varying levels of risks. You must balance these risks against your financial goals. If one of your goals is to keep a specific amount of money without any potential loss, you may deposit it in a savings account. If you want the potential to grow your money, you may decide to invest in stocks, mutual funds, or a business opportunity, understanding that you could lose some or all of your initial investment.

Regardless of the type of investment you choose, it's important that you understand what you're investing your money into. You must understand the specifics of each investment, how it has the potential to help you reach your Point B, and any risks involved. Your sole focus cannot be the potential money you could make. Do your homework before investing your money!

FINANCIAL COUNSELORS

Along with educating yourself, also speak with financial counselors who can assist you in developing short- and long-term financial goals. Financial counselors will provide you with several options for investing your money, but at the end of the day, it's still your money. Make sure your money is being invested in a manner that supports your Point B, and request a second (or third) opinion on any initial recommendations. Financial counselors don't have to live with their decisions in the long run—you do!

Be sure to do your homework on each counselor you speak with. Check his or her credentials, work history, and performance. Run a background check and learn whether he or she lives off commissions and fees or earns a standard salary. How counselors receive their income may influence their investment advice.

INVESTMENTS

The following pages provide an overview of several types of investments.

Savings Account: Backed by federal insurance, a savings account is a bank account that earns interest. Savings accounts have monthly transaction limits on withdrawals and outgoing transfers. Placing your money in a savings account is often considered a safe investment. However, the trade-off for safety is a low return of interest.

Certificates of Deposit: Backed by federal insurance, a certificate of deposit is a certificate issued by a bank where you deposit money for a specific period, while earning higher interest than savings and interest-bearing checking accounts.

Savings Bonds: Backed by the US government and issued in various values and types, savings bonds can earn interest as the bond matures. Savings bonds are not taxed at the state or local level and are postponed from federal tax until the bond is redeemed, reaches final maturity, or you give up ownership of the bond and it is reissued. For example, you purchase a one-hundred-dollar savings bond for fifty dollars. Interest accrues on the bond at a variable rate each month and compounds semiannually. You receive the interest income when you redeem the savings bond. Savings bonds mature to the face value of the bond at varying times based on the type and original purchase date.[1]

Corporate Bonds: With corporate bonds, you are loaning money (like an IOU) to a corporation for a predetermined period, from one to thirty years. In return, the corporation agrees to pay interest (called a coupon) on the loan amount (principle) until the bond matures. Corporate bonds provide a higher rate of return than government bonds.[2]

Mutual Funds: Mutual funds provide diverse investments (in stocks, bonds, and cash) without requiring investors to make separate purchases and trades. The money you (and others) invest into a specific mutual fund buys shares in the mutual fund. Each share represents part ownership in the fund and the income it generates. Mutual funds are managed by teams of professionals researching stocks, bonds, or other assets and then investing according to a specific plan or purpose. These professionals often charge an annual fee and other expenses.[3]

There are several types of mutual funds (money market, bond, stock, target date) that provide professional management, diversification, affordability, and liquidity (ability to redeem shares at any time, often within a few days).[4]

Stocks: A stock represents a share in the ownership of a company, offering you a claim on the company's assets and earnings. There are thousands of stocks available in various categories, such as size, style, and sector. Stocks can be purchased through brokerage firms for a set commission fee, though some brokerage firms provide no commission fees.[5]

Individual Retirement Accounts (IRAs): Established for retirement savings, IRAs are like savings accounts with tax benefits. There are two types of IRAs: traditional and Roth. With a traditional IRA, you typically pay taxes on the back end when you withdraw the money in retirement. Roth IRAs are the exact opposite. You pay taxes on the front end, not when you withdraw your money. However, your money will grow tax-free while in either IRA. Depending on the IRA, there may be limits for yearly contributions and penalties for early withdrawals.[6]

DIVERSIFICATION

Diversification is a risk-management principle that mixes a variety of investments within a portfolio (your total collection of investments) in order to minimize the impact any one investment can have on the overall performance of your portfolio. Basically, diversification is the act of not having all of your financial eggs in one basket.[7]

GIVE

Giving is an investment of your time, talents, or resources to assist another person, place, or thing without charging a fee or creating an obligation to repay.

Think of all the people who have made a positive impact in your life, large and small. The impact they made was through the giving of their time, talents, or resources. Because of their investment, your life improved in some way. They helped you reach a particular Point B in your life, even if it wasn't financial.

Each of us has a Point B, whether we've written it down or kept it in our thoughts and dreams. As many people gave their time, talents, and resources to help you get closer to your Point B, you can do the same for someone else. Your giving can ignite a spark of hope for a better and brighter future. The imprint you can leave on another's heart can be monumental. You can help someone's Point B become a reality.

See a need. Meet the need. Share your life with others.

CONCLUSION

High-Five Finances: Five Ways to Reach Your Financial Goals was written to help you get a better handle on your finances. It was tailored to meet you exactly where you are (financially) in order to help you build an individualized plan to address your short- and long-term needs and goals. From learning about your spending habits, being content with what you have, and even finding ways to protect yourself from yourself, I hope this journey has been beneficial for you, your family, and your finances.

It's never too late to get your financial house in order. Your future is too important. I hope *High-Five Finances: Five Ways to Reach Your Financial Goals* has been a catalyst for changing the direction of your life and finances for generations to come.

REFERENCES

1. FINRA. "US Savings Bonds." Financial Industry Regulatory Authority, Inc. Accessed September 29, 2015. http://www.finra.org/investors/us-savings-bonds.

2. FINRA. "Corporate Bonds." Financial Industry Regulatory Authority, Inc. Accessed September 29, 2015. http://www.finra.org/investors/corporate-bonds.

3. CNNMoney. "Mutual Funds: Investing in Mutual Funds." Cable News Network, A Time Warner Company. Accessed September 29, 2015. http://money.cnn.com/pf/money-essentials-mutual-funds/.

4. Investor.gov. "Mutual Funds." US Securities and Exchange Commission. Accessed September 29, 2015. http://investor.gov/investing-basics/investment-products/mutual-funds.

5. CNNMoney. "Stocks: How to Invest in Stocks." Cable News Network, A Time Warner Company. Accessed September 29, 2015. http://money.cnn.com/pf/money-essentials-stocks/.

6. CNNMoney. "Basics of an IRA: Ultimate Guide to Retirement." Cable News Network, A Time Warner

Company. Accessed September 29, 2015. http://
money.cnn.com/retirement/guide/IRA_Basics.moneymag/.

7. Investopedia. "Financial Concepts: Diversification."
Investopedia, LLC. Accessed September 29, 2015. http://
www.investopedia.com/university/concepts/concepts2.asp.

(com)mission™
PUBLISHING

www.commissionpubs.com
info@commissionpubs.com

www.ingramcontent.com/pod-product-compliance
Lightning Source LLC
Chambersburg PA
CBHW070948210326
41520CB00021B/7108